THE
CYCLOPES

MONSTERS OF MYTHOLOGY

25 VOLUMES

Hellenic
Amycus
Anteus
The Calydonian Boar
Cerberus
Chimaera
The Cyclopes
The Dragon of Beotia
The Furies
Geryon
Harpalyce
Hecate
The Hydra
Ladon
Medusa
The Minotaur
The Nemean Lion
Procrustes
Scylla and Charybdis
The Sirens
The Spear-birds
The Sphinx

Norse
Fafnir
Fenris

Celtic
Drabne of Dole
Pig's Ploughman

MONSTERS OF MYTHOLOGY

THE
CYCLOPES

Bernard Evslin

CHELSEA HOUSE PUBLISHERS

New York   New Haven   Philadelphia

1987

EDITOR
Jennifer Caldwell

ART DIRECTOR
Giannella Garrett

PICTURE RESEARCHER
Susan Quist

DESIGNERS
Carol McDougall, Noreen Lamb

CREATIVE DIRECTOR
Harold Steinberg

First Printing

Library of Congress Cataloging-in-Publication Data

Evslin, Bernard.
The cyclopes.

(Monsters of mythology ; bk. 1)
Summary: Describes the origins of the cyclopes,
their work as servants to the gods, and their memorable
encounter with Ulysses.
1. Cyclopes (Greek mythology)—Juvenile literature.
2. Polyphemus (Greek mythology)—Juvenile literature.
[1. Cyclopes (Greek mythology) 2. Polyphemus (Greek
mythology) 3. Mythology, Greek] I. Title. II. Series:
Evslin, Bernard. Monsters of mythology ; bk. 1.
BL820.C83E97   1987   398.2′1   86-24525

ISBN 1-55546-236-7

Printed i n Singapore

For my brave boy,

ELI BURBANK

who has met monsters and wants to meet more

Characters

Monsters

The Cyclopes (SY klahps) *sing.* (SY kloh peez) *plur.*	Huge one-eyed smiths; the eldest children of Uranus and Gaia
Hundred-handed Giants	Born of Mother Earth and her serpent lover
Dragons	Gigantic leather-winged, fire-breathing lizards grown from worms who fattened themselves upon the blood of the murdered Uranus
Brontes (BRAHN teez)	Cleverest of the Cyclopes; forged the first lightning bolt for Zeus
Polyphemus (pahl ih FEE muhs)	A cannibalistic Cyclops encountered by Ulysses

The Elder Gods

Uranus (u RAY nuhs)	Lord of the Sky and All Beneath; the Rain-giver
Gaia (GAY uh)	Mother Earth; wife to Uranus and mother of the Cyclopes, the hundred-handed giants, the Titans, and Cronos
Cronos (KROH nuhs)	Youngest of the Titans and king after Uranus; father of the Gods
Rhea (REE uh)	Sister and wife of Cronos; mother of Hestia, Demeter, Hades, Poseidon, Hera, and Zeus

The Pantheon

Zeus
(ZOOS)
King of the Gods after Cronos, and all powerful; wielder of thunder and lightning

Hera
(HEE ruh)
Sister and wife of Zeus; mother of Hephaestus and Ares

Hestia
(HEHS tih uh)
Elder sister of Zeus; Goddess of the Hearth

Demeter
(de MEE tuhr)
Sister of Zeus; Goddess of the Harvest

Hades
(HAY deez)
Brother of Zeus; King of the Land Beyond Death

Poseidon
(poh SY duhn)
Brother of Zeus; God of the Sea

Hephaestus
(he FEHS tus)
Eldest son of Zeus and Hera; the Smith God

Ares
(AIR eez)
Second son of Zeus and Hera; God of War

Athena
(uh THEE nuh)
Daughter of Zeus and the Titaness Metis; Goddess of Wisdom

Aphrodite
(af ruh DY tee)
Goddess of Love and Beauty; her name means foam-born

Apollo
(uh PAHL oh)
Son of Zeus and Leto; the sun God; also God of Music and Healing and Lord of the Golden Bow

Artemis
(AHR tuh mis)
Twin sister of Apollo; Goddess of the Moon and the Chase and Maiden of the Silvern Bow

Hermes
(HUR meez)
Son of Zeus and Maia; the Messenger God as well as God of Commerce; patron of liars, gamblers, and thieves

Heroes

Ulysses
(u LIHS eez)

King of Ithaca and leading strategist of the Greek forces in the war against Troy; he is the renowned voyager who survives a series of dreadful ordeals flung at him by the gods who sided with the Trojans

Others

Dione
(dy OH nee)

An oak dryad who aids Zeus

Leuce
(LOO say)

A river nymph who serves Cronos and maddens Polyphemus

Amalthea
(am uhl THEE uh)

Enormous she-goat who suckles the infant Zeus

Dryads
(DRY uhdz)

Wood nymphs

Naiads
(NAY uhdz)

Nymphs of those waters that are not the sea. They inhabit rivers, lakes, streams, fountains, and springs

Nereids
(ne REE uhdz)

Sea nymphs, all of them beautiful

Contents

1

The Maiming

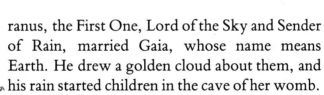ranus, the First One, Lord of the Sky and Sender of Rain, married Gaia, whose name means Earth. He drew a golden cloud about them, and his rain started children in the cave of her womb.

"Oh, my Lord," she cried, "these blessed babes of ours shall be the first born of love's embrace—creatures so wondrously beautiful that all must worship them."

"Beautiful, eh?" snarled Uranus to himself. "Then she may prefer them to me, me, me. Oh, no! Beautiful they shall not be, but so ugly that all will flee in horror."

Thereupon he cursed the first fruits of her womb, fashioning this curse into the shape of a bat, which he sent flying into the cave where the unborn infants lay. The bat plucked an eye from each head and ate them like grapes.

Mother Earth went into labor. The plains quaked. Mountains gushed fire. The ocean floor shook, starting tidal waves. When the sea withdrew, two children loomed on the wet beach, a boy and a girl. Giants they were, born full-grown, tall as trees and magnificently muscled.

But their father, hiding behind a storm cloud, smiled when he saw them. For each had but one eye set right in the middle of the forehead.

"A fine pair of monsters," chuckled Uranus to himself. "Not even their mother can love them."

But his troubles with their mother were just starting. She looked upon the monsters she had borne and knew somehow that it was Uranus who had made them the way they were. To avenge herself she went dancing on the flickering edge of creation and entertained a giant serpent. Shortly thereafter she gave birth to a litter of hundred-handed giants, whom she hid from sight in one of her deepest caves.

Her rage grew. Spasms of anger shook the earth. She wept tears of lava. Tidal waves were her tantrum. And Uranus could not approach her—not until he had vowed that from then on their children would be as beautiful as she had dreamed.

Sure enough, after they stopped quarreling, Gaia produced one child a year. Her brood, the Titans, were godlike in their beauty but of savage temper.

Now Mother Earth had many children, but she was troubled, for they were unkind to each other, and cruelest of all to her firstborn, whom their father had robbed of an eye each.

The huge single eye of the Cyclopes, glowing like a weird gem in the middle of their foreheads, struck terror into everyone who looked at them. Even the serpent's spawn, the hundred-handed giants who looked like enormous centipedes—even these hideous creatures disliked the sight of the Cyclopes and tried to avoid them. And the entire Titan tribe, who were very proud of their beauty, loathed the Cyclopes and kept planning ways to get rid of them forever, but didn't dare come close enough to attack.

Only Gaia, their mother, pitied them. Still, even she did not really relish the sight of them and managed to see as little of her firstborn as possible.

So, feared and shunned by everyone, the Cyclopes twins had only each other in all the new-made world. To say that they loved each other is to say too little. From the first, they were like two halves of the same body. They craved each other with a need that could not be satisfied. As far as possible they tried to *become* each other. They were two-eyed at such times, and although the eyes were in different heads, their vision was single. Coming so close, merging so utterly, they were able to forget the pain of being maimed and hated and isolated.

Time passed. Mother Earth began roaming her caves. She was with child again and feeling very special about this pregnancy because she knew it would be her last. Now she was looking for a place to bear her child. She went deeper than she had ever gone before, cavern beneath cavern beneath cavern, right into the entrails of the earth. She heard a curious mewing sound and held her torch high.

Among the thronging shadows she saw a huge jewel catching the torchlight, and fracturing it. She searched the shadows and saw that the jewel was an eye, the huge single eye of the girl

Spasms of anger shook the earth. Mother Earth wept tears of lava.

*Mother Earth began roaming her caves. . . . She heard
a curious mewing sound and held her torch high.*

Cyclops, brimming now with a great crystal tear. But the tear was of happiness. Crawling over her like kittens were four naked babes, each with a single eye in the middle of its forehead.

"Oh, horror, horror. . . . They're breeding true," murmured Earth to herself. "My blighted children are giving me blighted grandchildren. If they spawn like this, they will be as numerous as the Titans, who hate them so. They will turn, finally, upon their brothers and sisters. Heaven and earth will be torn by war. I must find some work for these terrible hands to do, some tools they can use instead of weapons."

She sank down upon the stone floor of the cave, took her daughter's ugly jeweled head onto her lap, and kissed her face. She gathered her grandchildren about her.

"These are fine children," she said. "They look just like you. You must lend them to me for a while. I shall teach them a skill that will keep them busy and happy all their days."

The little Cyclopes grew with monstrous speed and were full-grown in two months. When they came into their strength, Gaia led them among the mountains to a certain chasm where veins of greenish iron streaked the rocks. There, she taught them to quarry and smelt the ore. She gave them an old crater for their smithy. The smoldering volcanic flames were their forge fire; an enormous table stone, their anvil.

First, she taught them toolmaking: how to uproot trees, trim the trunks, and fit the great wooden shafts into lumps of iron, making huge sledgehammers. She was pleased to see they could use their brutal baling-hook fingers as daintily as a spider spinning a web. Under her instruction they learned to heat the ingots red-hot, lay them on their stone anvil, and shape them with the earth-shaking blows of their sledgehammers. And finally, they learned to work the metal as delicately as lace.

The Cyclopes made tools and weapons of iron—hammers, hooks, shovels, swords, spears, and knives. They made ornaments of tin and copper, silver and crystal, as well as lovely baubles of gold, diamonds, rubies, emeralds, and sapphires.

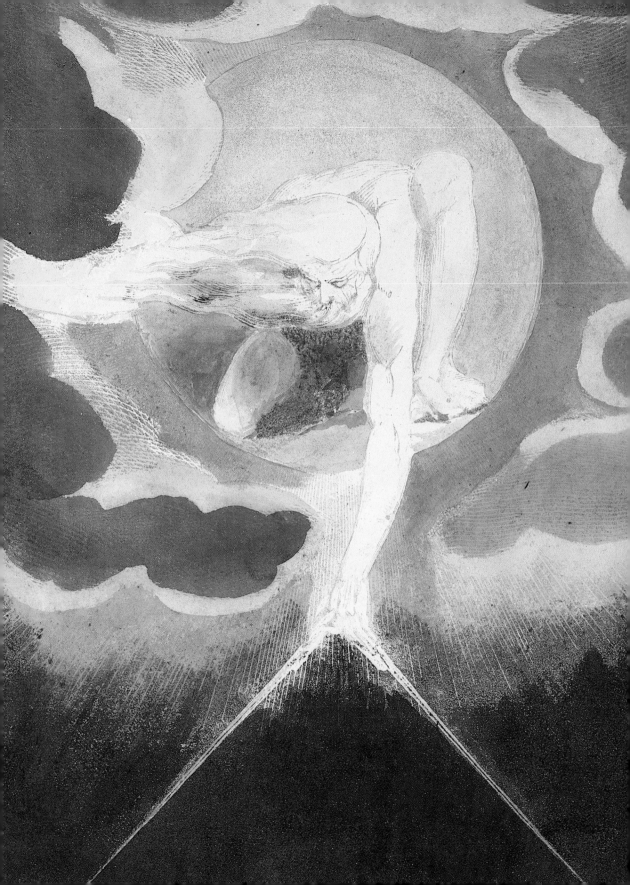

2

The Sickle

Gaia bore her child. He was called Cronos, and gave his name to Time.

Mother Earth favored her youngest son. She doted on him and he grew into a youth of blinding beauty. But she knew that her husband was growing jealous again.

She had Cronos meet her in a secret place and said, "Your father hates you, my boy."

"Why?"

"Because I love you too much."

"It is possible to love too much?"

"It is, and I do. And he hates you for it. And his hatred is a thing to dread. He robbed my first children of an eye each and made them so ugly they turned into monsters. Now he will rob you of your life."

"I am a god, you have told me. I cannot die."

"No, but you can be chopped into a hundred little pieces and buried in a hundred different places—and vanish from my sight as sure as death."

"He would do that to me?"

"Unless you do it to him first."

Cronos swung his sickle, shearing the head of Uranus from his body.

"You counsel me to chop my father into a hundred pieces?"

"As many as it takes, my son."

"He is very big and very powerful. The flash of his eye is lightning. His footfall is thunder. He shakes hurricanes out of his beard. How can I overcome him?"

"I have made certain preparations. The Cyclopes are as skillful as they are ugly; they work in metal. And I have had them forge an iron sickle sharp enough to cut through the hardest rock as if it were rotten wood—sharp enough to shear through the mighty bones of Uranus."

"What will he be doing while I'm swinging that sickle?"

"Trust me, Cronos. I have also had my smiths forge a chain of massive iron links. When you are ready to act—and it must be soon, soon—I'll whistle up your half brothers, the hundred-handed giants, who will take that chain and bind Uranus to the root of a mountain. Shackled to this granite pillar, he will be ready for dismemberment."

"Are you sure of this, mother?"

"Great enterprise requires great risk, my son. But I know your father, and, believe me, your peril is far greater if you don't do this than if you do. Think, think—would you rather be king of the gods, ruler supreme of heaven and earth, or a hundred bleeding gobbets of flesh scattered so wide and buried so deep that even I, for all my love, will not be able to gather you up and put you back together?"

Earth's children obeyed their mother. The Cyclopes forged and honed their iron sickle. Working furiously in the crater that was their smithy, they cast lumps of iron into the volcano's flames, drew out the red-hot ingots with iron tongs, laid them on the enormous slab of basalt that was their anvil, and hammered out massive rings, which they bent into each other until they had a chain strong enough to hold a god in his agony.

When sickle and chain were ready, Mother Earth whistled up her secret children, the hundred-handed giants. They came to her and she told them what to do.

That night, Uranus wrapped himself in a fleecy cloud and lay down to sleep on a plateau atop Mount Olympus. He awoke from a dream of falling to find himself actually underground in a dungeon cave of Tartarus, later to become the home of the dead. His massive body was chained to a granite pillar, and for all his titanic strength he could not break the links. Giant shapes stood guard. He recognized the glowing single eyes of the Cyclopes and realized with a terrible pang of grief that his mutilated children had risen against him. What a surprise, then, to see that his youngest son, the beautiful Cronos, was the one stepping toward him now, swinging a huge blade.

"Why you?" cried Uranus. "I have never harmed you."

"And never shall, dear father. My mother has taught me what to do."

"Spare me!" cried Uranus.

"Farewell," said Cronos. He swung his sickle, shearing the head of Uranus from his body.

As the head rolled in the dust, it spoke, saying: "You murder me now and take my throne. But a son of yours shall do the same to you. Live in fear, Cronos, for a severed head never lies."

3

The Betrayals

ow Cronos was king of the gods, Lord of the Sky and All Beneath, wielding awful power. Nevertheless, he could not forget those words uttered from the bloody dust and did indeed live in fear. The fear grew worse at night. He remembered it was at night that his father had been whisked from his mountain-top to the place of execution. So Cronos slept poorly and was tormented by nightmares. Finally, he complained to his mother.

"Get married," she said.

"Why?"

"A good wife brings dreamless sleep."

"My father thought he had a good wife, and look what happened to him."

"Ungrateful wretch!" shouted Gaia. "Do you dare reproach me? Me, your mother, who saved you from your father's deadly jealousy and showed you how to become king of the gods?"

"I'm sorry, mother. I know how much I owe to your loving care. Whom shall I marry?"

"There's only one wife for you—my strongest, wisest, most beautiful daughter, the goddess Rhea, who will become Mother Earth after me."

"Very well. Prepare the wedding."

For a while after his marriage Cronos slept soundly and did not dream. But then a thought hit him.

"Was it really wise to get married?" he muttered to himself. "Rhea will surely give me sons, and it was a son my father warned me against. Or am I jumping at shadows? My mother loves me best. Had there been danger in wedlock, she would never have made me marry. Nevertheless, there are certain steps I can take. After all, I needed powerful allies to dispose of my father. I'll see to it that no rebellious son of mine will have the same help."

Whereupon Cronos performed his second great act of treachery. He visited the crater smithy where the Cyclopes wrought their marvelous tools and weapons and ornaments. He stood on the anvil and spoke to the giant figures whose single eyes were like pits of red light in the flickering forge fires. And he made his voice as sweet as the wind blowing off the mountain to sing among the pines and cedars.

"Brothers, sisters, dear Cyclopes clan, I owe you a debt of gratitude that can never be paid. In my youth you helped me against my savage sire, who was bent on my destruction. I remember . . . I remember . . . and have always loved you for what you did on that night long ago. Now, dearest kinfolk, I am in danger again. Enemies plot against me. Once again I need the help that only you can give. Matchless smiths that you are, use your skill, I pray, to fashion an iron cage with bars so massively wrought that no creature in heaven, on earth, or beneath it, no leviathan that prowls the depths of the sea shall be able to break out of that cage once its gate is bolted. Brothers, sisters, will you once again help your king in his hour of need?"

Cronos knew this was the way to handle the great, simple-hearted brutes. He knew that they were so parched for affection, so raw inside from being disliked by everyone, that they would believe anything he said if he praised them first and pretended to like them.

They did believe him and were eager to please him. They worked night and day until they had built an enormous cage, strong enough to hold a herd of wild elephants. The Cyclopes sent word to Cronos that the cage was finished and ready to receive his enemies.

Cronos came to the smithy, but not alone. He had instructed the hundred-handed giants to follow him to the crater and wait hidden on the slope until he called them. He entered the smithy and laughed with joy when he saw the huge cage. It was set on

wheels, as he had asked, and its gate was bolted by an iron shackle whose link was as thick as the bars.

"Good work!" he cried. "But is it really as strong as it looks?"

"Stronger!" they shouted.

"Let's test it," he said. "It is very well known that you Cyclopes are the most powerful creatures in the entire world. If the cage can hold you, it can hold anyone. Please enter the cage, all of you. I'll chain the gate and you must try to break out. It's the only way to test what you have made."

The Cyclopes yelled and clanged their tools; they were

Cronos knew that the Cyclopes were so parched for
affection, so raw inside from being disliked by everyone,
that they would believe anything he said.

pleased with themselves. They filed into the cage laughing because they knew it was made so strong that even they, with all their volcanic force, could not escape. When the last one had entered, Cronos wrapped the chain around the sliding gate and stuck the great bolt through its links.

"Try to get out!" he called.

The Cyclopes flung themselves at the bars. They seized them with their enormous hands and tried to bend them. The bars held. Some of them had brought their sledgehammers inside. They swung the mallets, striking the bars, the gate and chain. Metal rang against metal in a hideous din. The very walls of the crater shook. But the cage held.

"It is strong, brother!" they called. "Stronger than strong! Now let us out. Open the gate and let us out."

No one answered. They peered through the bars and saw only the forge fire and the dancing red shadows. Cronos had vanished.

"Cronos!" they cried. "Brother! King! Come open the gate!"

Thick shapes blotted the shadows. They saw the hundred-handed giants slithering into the smithy like giant centipedes. Silently, the invaders reached with their hundred hands. Silently, they seized the cage and rolled it out of the crater and down a chain of rocky passages—down, down to the deepest cavern that lies at the root of the mountain called Olympus. And there they left the cage and its cargo of leaping, howling, weeping Cyclopes.

Midway up the cavern chain, they met Cronos coming down. "Oh, best of giants," he cried, "handiest of helpers! You have done me a great service this day. You have helped me rid myself of the monsters who dared plot against me. And now I shall reward you. Follow me down again and I shall lead you to my richest treasure vault, which is stacked high with bars of gold and chests of diamonds and rubies and emeralds. All shall be yours!"

Greedily, the giants followed him. They didn't know that they, in turn, were being followed. They were so drunk with visions of treasure that they didn't realize they were being trailed down the rocky tunnel by a band of Titans, those elder brothers of Cronos, who had become his court and served him in all ways.

Cronos led the giants down to a cave that had a narrow mouth but widened suddenly into a great chamber. It was just one level up from where the Cyclopes were penned—close enough, indeed, so that the giants could hear a faint shrieking as it drifted up through the rock floor. But they paid no heed. They rushed into the dark chamber, which grew darker still as the Titans came racing down the tunnel and rolled an enormous boulder across the mouth of the cave.

The giants milled about in the vanishing light, stunned that Cronos, who had used them to imprison the Cyclopes, was now imprisoning them.

But the realization grew. They knew they were being sealed up in the bowels of the earth. They raged and frothed, leaped and shouted. They pounded at the rock until their many hands were lumps of bloody gristle. But the rock stood against their blows. The Titans trundled other boulders down the tunnel, wedging them against the first great rock that blocked the portal, until the whole corridor was choked with boulders and the only way to free the captives would be to tear the mountain up by its roots.

4

The Cannibal God

With the Cyclopes and the giants now buried beneath tons of earth, Cronos slept peacefully again. But after a while he began to hear a faint shrieking at night. It seemed to be seeping out of the earth and floating up to the top of Mount Olympus, and he realized that the caged Cyclopes and the sealed-up giants must be howling underground.

"Ridiculous," he said to himself. "Why should I let these sounds bother me? They can't get out no matter how they howl."

After some time the howling stopped, or he stopped hearing it, and Cronos almost forgot his prisoners. But now mighty oaks had grown from certain patches of earth where pieces of Uranus were buried, and when the wind blew, the oak leaves seethed, murmuring: "Beware, Cronos, beware. . . ."

In his sleep, Cronos heard the trees talking, and he was seized again by nightmare—which grew worse when Rhea told him she was pregnant.

"Will our firstborn be a son?" he whispered to himself. "Is this the one who will try to overthrow me as my father foretold?

Hah! I'll give the seditious brat no chance. If it's a boy, I'll drown him like a kitten. A daughter I may let live, for I am tender-hearted.''

But when his first child appeared, Cronos was in such a hurry to get rid of it that he didn't wait to find out whether it was a boy or a girl, nor did he take the time to drown it. He simply swallowed it whole, as a cat swallows a grasshopper. It all happened so quickly that Rhea believed him when he told her that the infant had been born dead and that he had swiftly disposed of it so that she would not be saddened by the sight of the tiny corpse.

And she believed him the second time she gave birth and the babe vanished. She half believed him the third time. But by the fourth time she was growing mistrustful. She tried to fight against her suspicions. Her husband was displaying greater grief at the loss of each child, and this confused her.

Then her fifth infant vanished before she could hold it in her arms. Cronos, weeping, told her that this one had also been born dead and that he had quickly burned the body to save her from distress. This time she found she could not believe him. He was sobbing loudly but his eyes were gleaming, and not with tears. Besides, she realized that he seemed a little fatter after each child vanished.

Rhea went to old Mother Earth and told her tale. "I have been wondering about this," said Gaia. "All the rest of my Titan brood is very fertile; they have given me hundreds of grandchildren—big, beautiful ones. You and Cronos alone have given me none."

"Oh, mother, what shall I do?"

"Send Cronos to me."

Cronos came to her and she said, "Have you been murdering your children?"

"They were born dead. Didn't Rhea tell you?"

"She told me much. Now you must tell what it means."

"Well, mother, your youngest daughter, the wife you chose

for me, seems incapable of producing a live infant. But I'll pretend no grief. For you must know what my father foretold with his last breath: that a son of mine would do to me what I was doing to him."

"Then you *have* been killing them?"

"No need. They were born dead."

"You're a liar, my son."

"I am king. The truth is what I say it is."

"Cronos, I have loved you well, too well. For your sake I have committed crimes. I taught you to defend yourself against a murderous, evil father, thinking that your beauty was a sign of goodness and that you would reign justly and wisely over the boiling seas and the new-made earth and all the different kinds of things coming in to being. Now, alas, I see you turning into the very image of your bloody father. Stop, son. Stop, now! Don't devour your children. Let them live and grow. And I shall forgive you. Rhea will forgive you. The blessings of the earth and its fountains shall be upon you. And you shall reign happily and well."

"I am king, mother."

"So was your father."

"I am king and intend to remain king. I am the one to forgive or condemn, to bless or curse, to bestow life or death, as I please."

Gaia left him and went to Rhea. "You must be brave, my daughter," she said. "There is a way to save your next child, but it will require a great deal of courage on your part."

"Tell me what to do."

"When you become pregnant again, pretend you're not until you can no longer conceal your condition. Then lie to him about the date so that he won't be expecting you to go into labor until some time after you actually do. No one will know the truth except you and me. I shall attend your labor and be your midwife, and when the child is born, I shall take it to a safe place. Afterward, you will tell your husband that you have miscarried."

"But my child, my first live one, how can I bear not to have it with me?"

"You shall visit him every day. I promise."

"Will it be a boy?"

"Yes."

"How do you know?"

"I can't tell you, but I will tell you this: when I know something without knowing how, it always comes true. If we properly deceive your husband, you shall have a son and a mighty one—the next king of the gods, if all goes well."

On the night that Rhea knew her baby was to be born, she crept out of the garden of Olympus and followed her mother down a moonlit slope to a grove of oaks. She saw light splintering among the hulking shadows; it was a golden cradle hanging from the tallest tree, glittering as it swung, as if the new moon itself had dropped from the sky and had been caught in the branches.

"That cradle is for the child you will bear tonight," said Gaia.

"It's lovely here," said Rhea, "but quite close to Olympus. Suppose Cronos stumbles on this place while hunting?"

"I have chosen carefully," said Gaia. "These oaks spring from the butchered body of your father. Their taproots drink of his vengeful blood. And so the trees have learned to hate Cronos, and will stand sentinel for us. Should he approach, every loud crow that nests in these branches will cry a warning and I shall hide the child before he comes. Enough talk now. It is time for you to bear your son."

Rhea squatted on the great white pillars of her thighs. Her hair was a net of moonlight. Her bare feet clutched the ground. Gaia pressed her belly and caught the child as it slid out.

Shouting with glee, she held him to the sky. A west wind arose, making the moon rock like a boat. Stars danced. Night birds rejoiced.

Gaia gazed at her daughter. "We'll have to change our

"These oaks spring from the butchered body of your father. . . . The trees have learned to hate Cronos, and will stand sentinel for us."

plan," she said. "Cronos will never believe that you had a miscarriage. You look too happy."

"I can't help it, mother. I *am* too happy."

"Yes, and as soon as as he sees you, he'll understand what has happened and will begin to hunt for the child."

"What shall we do?"

Gaia snatched up a rock and wrapped it in a white cloth. "Go to him, holding this to your breast as if you were suckling a babe."

"First let me hold my son. Isn't he the most beautiful thing you've ever seen?"

"Yes."

"My marriage almost killed me mother. But I'm alive again. Alive! This babe is the breath of life to me. I name him Zeus."

This meant breath in their language.

"Zeus he is and shall be. Go now daughter. Take up your rock and go. Trick your husband and save your child."

Cronos awoke from a deep sleep to see Rhea approaching. Her face was radiant; she held a white bundle to her breast and

Gaia held the baby to the sky. A west wind arose. . . . Stars danced.

was humming a lullaby. Cronos leaped from the great bed, snorting and bellowing. He snatched the bundle from her and swallowed it clothes and all.

The stone lay heavily upon him and he thought: "Curse it, this is one solid brat she dropped. He sits on my gut like a rock. Undoubtedly, he was the one destined to make trouble, and she tried to hide him from me, the treacherous bitch! Well, never again. I'll find a way to get rid of her, too."

5

Zeus

Rhea didn't dare inflame her husband's suspicions by going to the grove too often or staying long enough to suckle her babe. So Gaia employed wet nurses—two nymphs who had recently given birth. One of them was a wood nymph named Melissa who belonged to the bee clan; her breasts ran with honey. The other, Lacta, was a meadow nymph, and the baby god drank rich milk from her breasts. So huge was his appetite, though, that he had soon sucked the nymphs dry and his grandmother had to import a she-goat.

The goat's name was Amalthea. Larger than any cow, she had a pelt of tightly curled fur, white as cloud fleece. Her eyes were slanted pools of yellow light; her horns, silvery gold as the new moon. Three nipples ran with milk, three ran with honey, and she never went dry. She not only suckled the young Zeus but allowed him to ride her like a horse. She swam with him, stood under the trees when he climbed them, and guarded him while he slept. She was the first creature he ever loved, and there was no one he ever loved more.

Now the godling had a quality that not even his doting mother or his wise old grandmother could appreciate. He was born with a sense of kingship that gave each of his senses imperial power. He claimed everything that touched his awareness: tree,

Amalthea was the first creature Zeus ever loved,
and there was no one he ever loved more.

nymph, spider, fish, cat, raindrop, wind, star, mudhole. Nothing was too big, too small, too wet, too dry, too old, or too young. Everything fascinated him; nothing disgusted him or made him afraid.

Zeus learned that he could do more with his eyes than see. His gaze carried the essence of himself along the line of his sight and seized all that he looked upon. He could make pebbles dance. As he grew, he made rocks move. They wrenched themselves out of their sockets of earth to roll after him. By simply looking at birds, he could make them motionless, then loose them again to fly in circles about his head.

All this time, Cronos, who was as patient as he was crafty, kept watching Rhea very closely. He also sent his Titan courtiers out daily, spying in all directions, until finally one came to him with a disturbing report. Cronos sent for Rhea and said: "I hear of a magical child roaming the woods—a boy, very handsome and supple as a sapling. Do you know anything about him?"

"No, my lord."

"You know, wife, I had a dream about this. I saw the lad running across a field and a boulder rolling after him like a pet dog. You were standing beside me, watching, and when I asked you about him, you said: 'Boy? What boy? There's no boy here.' See how you are? Always lying."

"I cannot help what you dream. I know nothing of such a lad. Are you sure he exists? Have you seen him when you were awake?"

"There are those who have."

"Perhaps he is of the Titan brood? A nephew of ours, then?"

"Nonsense! Any such child would have been introduced at court, you know that. Rhea, something is wrong. Something dwells in the forest and has become a menace to me. I shall go hunting tomorrow. I'll take my hounds, who can track down any game, and my spear that never misses its mark. I'll run him like a deer, whoever he is, and cut him down when he's brought to bay."

Rhea fled the garden of Olympus and sought her mother. "Hide my son!" she cried. "Do it now. His father comes a-hunting!"

And she sobbed out her tale.

"The boy will be hidden deep, deep . . ." said Gaia. "But only long enough for Cronos to grow unwary. Then we must take action to end this terror."

She called Zeus to her and said, "You must leave this place and go underground."

"For how long?"

"Until your father decides that you don't exist."

"What shall I do underground?"

"Learn what lies beneath, for it is also part of your realm-to-be, and not the least part. Explore its caves, its buried rivers, the roots of mountains. Observe the veins of iron and copper and tin. Study jewels that look like lumps of coal until the eyes grow wise. Look upon giant worms, wintering serpents, and twisted demons who reside in the clefts of rocks and shall serve you when you have founded death's domain. But, most importantly, you must visit your impounded kinsfolk—the Cyclopes, in their terrible cage, and the walled-up giants of a hundred hands. Go to them, learn their grief, judge the heat of their rage, and think how to befriend them. For it is these monsters who will help you establish your kingdom. Go, grandson, go under now. I shall send you word when it is safe to return."

Cronos assembled a hunting party of Titans. He ordered out his pack of hounds. Specially bred to serve him on the chase, they were white as arctic wolves but with golden manes and plumed golden tails. They were swift enough to overtake a stag, powerful enough to pull it down in mid-stride, and had noses keen enough to follow a track three weeks old.

Horses had not yet been created, but Cronos and his Titans could run tirelessly all day long, and almost as swiftly as their hounds.

Indeed, this hunt lasted for a day and a night, and into a second day. Cronos made his party search every copse, every grove, every stand of river reed. They foraged up every slope of every hill on the Olympian range and entered every cave, but they found no trace of the boy. Cronos was in a savage mood when he returned to his palace.

He was very weary after the hunt, but he could not sleep. He tossed and turned, then finally realized what was keeping him awake. It was the silence. The howling had stopped. For the first time since he had caged the Cyclopes and trapped the giants, he did not hear their shrieking as it rose through layers of rock and drifted faintly on the wind to Olympus. It must be understood that screams of pain are a tyrant's lullaby.

"Why don't I hear them?" he muttered to himself. "Can they have broken out? No . . . impossible! They must simply have grown so weak that they can utter no sound. Or, perhaps, since they are given no food, they have devoured each other and there is no one left."

He kept trying to comfort himself. Nevertheless, he could not sleep. He arose and began to prowl the corridors of the cloud castle. He was boiling with unfocused rage. He needed to hurt someone and he knew who that someone was. This was the night to punish his wife for all the unwanted infants she had borne, especially that last one who still lay like a stone in his belly.

He ran to the wall where his sickle hung. He lifted it down and swung it lightly, smiling. "A bit rusty," he said to himself, "but sharp enough to slice that pestiferous wife of mine into as many pieces as it did my father."

Holding the sickle, he strode toward the far wing of the castle where Rhea slept. But living with a murderous husband had taught her to be a light sleeper. She had trained herself to pick up the vibrations of his wrath even as she slept. Now, when she heard his heavy footsteps and the clank of iron, she knew it was time to leave.

She slipped out of her bed, ran into the garden, and slid like a shadow through the trees and down the slope. She listened for sounds of pursuit but heard nothing.

"Mother . . . mother," she she called softly. She didn't dare

"I hear of a magical child roaming the woods—
a boy, very handsome and supple as a sapling."

"Learn what lies beneath. . . . Look upon giant worms, wintering serpents, and twisted demons who reside in the clefts of rocks.

raise her voice, nor did she have to. Gaia fledged herself out of the darkness. She came in the form of an enormous crone. Her hair hung like the vine called silver lace, and her eyes were slits of moonlight.

"Mother . . . mother," whispered Rhea. "My husband has taken up his sickle. He means me terrible harm."

"Yes, daughter, it's time for you to vanish for a while."

"Where shall I go?"

"Follow your son underground."

"Nothing would give me more joy. But he is so fiery, so proud, the little love. Would he welcome a mother trailing after him on his first adventure?"

"He will be able to use your help. He has much to do down there. He will be freeing your maimed brothers and sisters. Yes, I mean the Cyclopes, blighted first by their father's jealousy, then imprisoned by their brother's fear."

"He buried them deep. How many times have I listened to him boast about locking the Cyclopes in their own cage? What can my son do? He's only half-grown."

"And will grow no older unless we get rid of his father."

"But can we? How?"

"The first step is to free the Cyclopes. They will serve us well in the dreadful war that is to come. Go down to your son now; stay with him until I recall you both."

Meditation On an Oak Leaf (1942) by Andre Masson

6

Underground

ot only prophetic oaks sprouted from the murdered Uranus, whose body had been chopped into small pieces and buried in many different places. Worms gathered too. They swarmed in a great, greedy tangle to drink his blood. They tunneled into the massive shards of his bones, fed on the rich marrow, and grew huge.

As they feasted on the god who had been cut up alive, they became filled with his unspent wrath. Envenomed through every cell of their bodies, they primed themselves for murder. Clothing themselves in leather scales as tough as armor plate, they grew teeth like ivory blades and spiked tails that could knock down trees. Finally, to become utterly destructive, they sprouted great leather wings and taught themselves to blow jets of flame out of their gullets.

So it was that a generation of dragons sprang out of the butchered god and grew into the very embodiment of spite. They became a breed of monster that was to form a taste for heroes and torment humankind for the next thousand years.

Now, young Zeus, while exploring a chain of caverns, came upon a dragon den. Separate dens, really. Except for one night a year, which was set aside for mating, no two dragons could meet without trying to kill each other. When the young were hatched out of the great green eggs, mother dragons kept them away from other adults, who liked to eat their young, just like Cronos.

Zeus wedged himself into a cleft of rock and hid there, observing his first dragon. He didn't know that these beasts had grown from the maggots that had fed themselves fat on the blood and bones of his buried grandfather. Though he felt no kinship to the scaly brutes, he studied them with great interest. He was especially struck by the way the dragons spouted flame. For some reason, this fascinated him beyond its own uniqueness. He knew this deadly trait was important to him, but he didn't know why.

He made his way to the Cyclopes' cage. He slipped into the chamber silently. Now, these early gods were not easily moved to sympathy. They kept their compassion for themselves and did not really feel the sufferings of anyone else. But when young Zeus looked through the bars into the cage and saw those gigantic figures standing as still as trees, their eyes blazing into the darkness—when he saw them looming there, so huge and patient, like penned cattle—he felt a strange tugging in his chest that he didn't know was pity. Their single blazing eyes misted over and big tears welled up until they overflowed and fell hissing onto the cage floor. Zeus saw those lava-hot tears, smelled the salt steam of them, and realized that these kinfolk of his had been standing here in the darkness for many years. He felt his own eyes getting wet and realized that for the first time in his life he was weeping. Then and there he knew what he would try to do.

He turned away from the cage and entered a rocky corridor. There, he leaned against a wall and looked at the floor. He stared

steadily at a pile of pebbles until they began to stir. The pile broke. Pebbles came rolling toward him. Faster and faster they rolled, leaping and turning in the air. He looked away and the pebbles dropped. He stared at a fist-sized stone. It did not move. He stared hard and saw the stone twitch. It rose into the air, fell, and came skipping toward him. He looked away and it stopped.

He turned his gaze on a medium-sized rock that was half-buried. It sat there motionless. He glared at it, pouring his will along the line of his sight. He saw the rock rise from its bed of earth, tearing itself free, shedding clumps of dirt. He made it rise straight up and hang in the air, then blinked and let it fall back into its hole.

Now he was ready. Singing and shouting, he raced along the dark corridor until he came to a passageway that was blocked by boulders. He knew that beyond this place the hundred-handed giants had been trapped.

He saw that the rocks clogging the passageway were not socketed in earth, but were a kind of huge rubble; they had been wedged in together, leaning on each other. He studied the formation and selected a certain boulder—not the nearest one, not the largest one, but a rock that was central to the mass. He fixed his gaze on it and stared until he felt his eyes popping out of his head. It sat there, massive and motionless.

Zeus sent his mind back along the seedbed of ancestral memory, back to when the earth was a white-hot coal spinning on the edge of chaos, cooling into red-hot rock. In the deep fertile crags and valleys of the young god's mind, stone became liquid, and his gaze began to soften the rock he looked upon. It softened; it trembled like jelly. That ponderous boulder, central to the mass, quivered, shook, shifted—loosening the entire rock jam. Tons of rock came sliding out of the corridor, faster and faster, in a terrific cataract of stone.

Zeus leaped out of the way, or he would have been crushed like an insect. He watched the rocks clatter past. The passageway was clear; and the cave mouth was a black hole. Out of that hole slithered what looked like a gigantic centipede. It was one of the giants, crawling on his hands, blinking in the dusty light.

"Come out!" cried Zeus. "You are free!"

The other giants came crawling out of the cave and squatted in the passageway, blinking at the young god.

"You are free," he said. "It is I who have ended your captivity. I, Zeus, your kinsman and your king-to-be, if you help me now."

"Hail!" they shouted. "All hail to you, oh liberator! We shall serve you in any way you wish."

In the deep fertile crags and valleys of the
young god's mind, stone became liquid, and his gaze began
to soften the rock he looked upon.

"Come, then. A perilous task awaits. And I have need of your many strong hands."

He led them at a run down the cavern chain. The giants were so big that they had to stoop, or their heads would have scraped the cave roofs. Startled bats wheeled in a cloud, chittering. He led the giants to the dragon den. Before entering, he gathered them about him and told them what they were to do.

They entered the den. It was littered with bones, for the dragons went up at night to hunt and dragged their kill back to their cave. A gust of blue lit the den as the dragon came to meet them, not yet spitting flame, but softly exhaling it. The many-handed ones were huge, and their wavering shadows even larger, but they looked small beside the looming beast—as small as ducks facing an alligator.

"Now!" cried Zeus.

The giants flung themselves on the dragon, which was frozen by surprise, for nothing ever attacks a dragon. Before it could recover, it was clamped by hundreds of hands with fingers stronger than baling hooks.

The giants, obeying their instructions, lofted the dragon high over their heads and held it there as they raced along the corridor. It was spitting fire, but its head was tilted firmly upward and the flame of its breath was going straight up, singeing bats on the wing.

With a mighty shout that bounced off the cave walls and redoubled, echoing, Zeus led the giants and their living torch to the place where, so many years before, they had wheeled the Cyclopes' cage. And there in the cage towered the Cyclopes. Dragon fire lit up their great, single eyes.

The giants had their instructions. Swiftly and expertly, they handled the dragon, wielding it as a welder does his torch. Using the beast's fiery breath, they aimed his blue flame on the bolt of the chain that bound the gate.

The big shackle grew red-hot, then white-hot, then melted away. The chain clanged to the floor, the gate slid open. The

*A gust of blue lit the den as the dragon came to
meet him, not yet spitting flame, but softly exhaling it.*

Cyclopes streamed out of the cage; they fell on their knees before Zeus.

He raised his voice and said: "Good Cyclopes, worthy giants, I who have brought you freedom now promise you vengeance. Your enemy is my enemy, and we shall fight him together. Yes, we shall wage war upon the tyrant Cronos and his Titan court. But to fight is not enough; we must also win. So we must prepare for this war. I bid you remain underground for a time. You, Cyclopes, shall search the caverns until you find a live crater to be your smithy. Stoke the volcanic flames that will be your forge fire. Swing your hammers in my service. Make an armory of weapons. But to forge these weapons you will need metal. You will need iron and copper. And this the giants will provide. They will dig and delve with their many mighty hands and tear the raw metal from the very entrails of the earth. And when the war is over and I come into my kingship, no one, I vow, will stand closer to the throne than you, my brothers and sisters. Yes, so high shall be your estate that your blemishes will be viewed as marks of privilege and everyone will regret not having been born with a single eye or a hundred hands."

7

Family Reunion

While Zeus was underground, Gaia employed certain serpents to go down and tell her what was happening below. Upon the evening of the twenty-first day, one such serpent reported the liberation of the Cyclopes. Mother Earth shouted with joy and went to seek Cronos.

She said, "My mother's instinct tells me that you are troubled by indigestion."

"A feeble term for what I suffer," said Cronos. "Something sits on my gut like a rock."

"Something you ate, no doubt?"

"No doubt, mother. No doubt."

"I can help you, son. A wood nymph of my acquaintance has found certain herbs that can cure the worst stomach ache."

"Go fetch her. I'll try anything."

Far underground a topaz-eyed snake slithered toward Zeus, put its leathery head to the youth's ear, and whispered dryly: "I am sent by your grandmother. Her message is: 'We strike tomorrow!'"

All night Zeus climbed up through the cavern chain, and dawn found him with Gaia. She took him into her huge embrace and said, "Today is the day, if all goes well, that you lose a father and gain some brothers and sisters."

"You've been busy," said Zeus.

"So have you, my boy. You have done great deeds below, and now that you have provided us with such strong allies, we can open hostilities."

"I'm ready," said Zeus.

"Clothe yourself in these rags and put on this wig of straw. You are to transform yourself into a bumpkin who has fallen in love with a beautiful wood nymph—so violently, so helplessly in love that your poor wits are quite addled. You have gone mute and can moan only 'Dione . . . Dione,' which is her name, and follow her about, begging with your eyes."

"An undignified role, grandmother."

"You'll be able to afford dignity after you gain your throne, grandson. Now hearken. Disguised as this love-sodden swain, you shall attend the nymph when I bring her to meet Cronos. You shall remain in the background, but stand ready to act when I give the word."

"Instruct me, Earth."

Clad in rags and wearing a wig of straw, the tall young god listened carefully as Gaia told him what to do.

Now it is known that those who are most careful about themselves are precisely those who will submit to the most brutal treatment as long as it is recommended by someone who supposedly knows something about health. This has been going on since the beginning of time, and started with Cronos and his bellyache. The king of the gods had a completely suspicious nature. He mistrusted everyone, especially his family. He also loathed strangers. He surrounded himself with Titan guards and never ate until a slave had tasted the food, lest it be poisoned. He imprisoned and executed anyone who looked at him the wrong way. And yet, he was ready to believe his mother, whom he mistrusted even more than he did his wife, when she told him that a wood nymph had mixed certain herbs that would cure the griping pain in his gut.

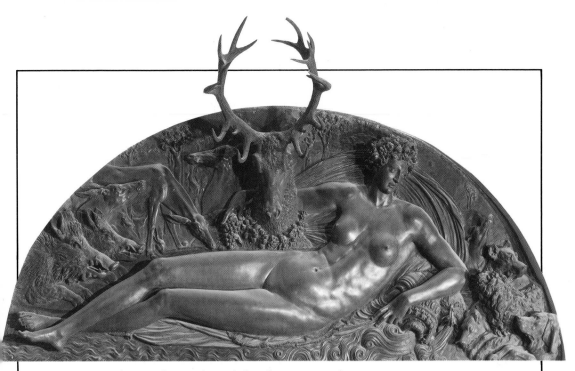

The wood nymph smiled at him so sweetly,
and looked so long-legged and lovely in
her brief costume, that Cronos was charmed.

He stood now on a sunny meadow, waiting. He saw his enormous mother trundling toward him over the grass, followed by two figures. One was a wood nymph clad only in leaves. Behind her came a shambling, slack-mouthed fellow with a thatch of straw-colored hair. He carried a keg and a flagon, and Cronos took him for a servant.

"All hail, king of the gods!" cried Gaia. "This is the dryad, Dione, come to ease your pain."

"Glory, glory," murmured the nymph in a voice that was like the west wind sighing through the treetops. "If by my poor woodland skills I am privileged to serve our beloved king, I shall count myself the proudest, happiest dryad in the entire forest."

And she smiled at him so sweetly, and looked so long-legged and lovely in her brief costume, that Cronos was charmed and quite forgot that he had meant to have one of his Titans taste her potion first to make sure it wasn't poisoned.

"Come, pour!" said Gaia.

Whereupon the nymph's servant swung the keg from his shoulder and poured purple wine into the flagon. Cronos was amazed by the lad's strength. He handled the heavy keg one-handed, as if it were a pitcher. He passed the flagon to the dryad, who took a pouch from her girdle and dusted some powder into the wine. Kneeling, she offered the great flagon to Cronos, holding it out with both hands. He took it and lifted it to his lips.

Sun-ripened Attic grapes had been pressed for this wine, which was then aged in oak for a hundred years. Such a wine was always mixed with water, but this was undiluted. It was so strong that it quite hid the flavor of what the nymph had put into

it—mustard and salt, mashed up with putrefying frogs' eggs.

Cronos drank down the entire flask in one gulp.

The earth tilted. Cronos braced himself between two trees and began to heave, a terrible, dry retching.

"The medicine is trying to work, my lord," said Dione. "It needs a bit of assistance."

"Now!" cried Gaia.

Zeus hiked his tunic, baring a long, sinewy thigh. He pivoted on his heel and, with all the terrific leverage of his immortally powerful young body, kicked his father in the belly.

Cronos doubled over and began to vomit. He spewed up first the stone he had swallowed, then each of his five children, who, being gods, were undigested and still alive. They came out in reverse order of the way

Zeus hiked his tunic, baring a long, sinewy thigh.

they had been swallowed—the youngest first. This was a girl, Hera. Next came a boy, Poseidon. Then another girl, Demeter. Then another boy, Hades. And finally the eldest child, a daughter named Hestia.

Residing in the great belly, they had grown to child-size. Now, as they breathed the golden air, they immediately gained the full strength of their radiant youth and danced about their fallen father, shouting and singing.

"Brothers and sisters!" cried Zeus. "Welcome to the world!"

He had cast off rags and wig and stood revealed as himself. The young gods embraced him. Hera clung to him, kissing his face again and again.

"You saved us!" she cried. "You are the youngest of us all, but the bravest and the strongest and the wisest. You shall be our king!"

His two other sisters cried, "Yes, yes, you must be our king!"

Poseidon grinned falsely and nodded. Black-browed Hades, the eldest brother, looked very somber, but said nothing.

"You shall be our king now," cried Hera. "And my husband later!"

"I shall serve as your war chief now," said Zeus, "and king later, if we win. Brothers, sisters, you are under orders. Catch the old king! Bind him fast!"

But when they turned to obey, they gaped in astonishment. For Cronos, who had been sprawled unconscious on the meadow, was no longer there. Only Zeus understood what must have happened. From the depths of his swoon Cronos had realized his peril, and with his matchless talent for survival had summoned a last desperate magic and made himself vanish.

8

The Magic Weapons

eus visited the smithy where the Cyclopes were making weapons. With him was his sister Hera. When they entered the crater, they knew something was wrong. The iron music of the anvils had fallen silent. They heard angry shouts and the sound of scuffling. A party of Cyclopes came to Zeus dragging a young smith, bound hand and foot.

"He has gone mad, oh Lord," said the head smith. "He refuses to work at his appointed task and, when questioned, will answer only in the wildest fashion about his hammer telling him something, and about something else he saw in the flames."

"Question him yourself," whispered Hera to Zeus.

Zeus spoke directly to the captive. "What is your name?"

"I am Brontes."

"Why are you acting this way?"

"I am doing what I must."

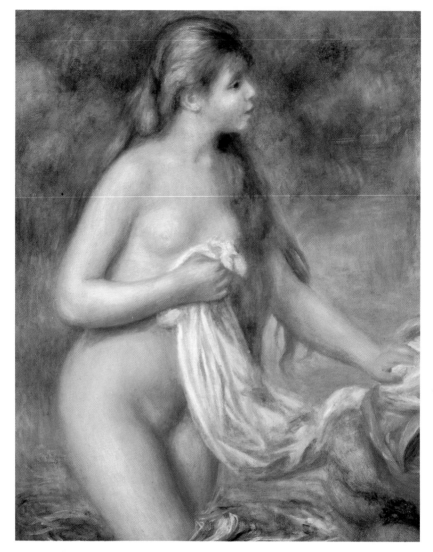

*From the depths rose a lovely water nymph, naked
and dripping. She climbed onto the bank and listened.*

Zeus spoke softly to Hera. "It's the dreadful heat and the
incessant din. It's a wonder more of them don't go crazy."

"I don't think he's crazy," said Hera. "Make him talk."

Zeus said, "Brontes, tell me exactly what happened."

"Exactly this," said Brontes. "When I started work this

morning, my sledgehammer jumped in my hands and danced on the anvil, beating out a song:

> Light above,
> Dark beneath.
> To vanquish the sire
> Staff with three teeth,
> And spear of fire.

"Does it have a meaning?" asked Zeus.

"I looked into the forge fire," said Brontes. "In the core of the flame I saw pictures form. A brass helmet like an overturned bowl, spilling darkness. A three-tined staff, or trident. Your brother Hades held the helmet. Your brother Poseidon wielded the trident."

"How about the spear of fire?"

"A thunderbolt!" shouted Brontes. "For you, oh Zeus. Weapon now, scepter to be."

Zeus turned to Hera, "What do you think?"

"Helmet of darkness," she murmured. "Trident. Thunderbolt. Could these be the weapons to defeat Cronos? Perhaps this one-eyed fellow has been granted special insight. Perhaps he has been chosen to receive a message from the very center of mystery."

"Perhaps," said Zeus. "That crazed song has the ring of truth. I thank you, Brontes, and commission you to make this magical gear: a helmet of darkness, a trident, and a thunderbolt. Above all, my thunderbolt! Do that first."

Cronos, whose spies were everywhere, soon learned that the Cyclopes were forging magical weapons to ensure his defeat.

"This must not be," he said to himself. "I'll have to think of a way to stop production."

When Cronos was threatened, he thought quickly. He stood on a riverbank and whistled in a certain way. From the depths rose a lovely water nymph, naked and dripping. She climbed onto the bank and listened, smiling, as he told her what he wanted.

"What will you give me if I do?" she said.

. . . ignoring the whole affair, Brontes was working stubbornly, and by this time had finished the helmet of darkness.

"The question that should concern you," growled Cronos, "is what you'll get if you don't."

The crater was so smoky that no one saw the naiad come in. She glided to the center of the great chamber and jumped on an anvil. Standing there, clad only in her long hair, she glimmered like a white birch. And like a tree casting a shadow, she spread a riverine coolness through the sweltering crater. A low, hungry moaning arose from the male Cyclopes as they moved slowly toward her.

Now the female Cyclopes always worked alongside the males, handling the same hot ingots and swinging the same heavy sledgehammers. They were as large and powerful as the males, and as dangerous in any kind of fight.

Shrieking with rage, they attacked the males with swinging mallets. Many of the males had dropped their hammers and were helpless against the savage assault. They fled. Some of them were caught and brutally beaten. Others were thrown into the fire pit and were badly charred before they could climb out.

Two of the females charged the anvil where the naiad stood, meaning to do such dreadful things to her that no nymph would ever again try to steal their mates. But it is almost impossible to catch a naiad—or any kind of nymph who doesn't want to be caught. This one simply melted into the shadows and vanished.

It was upon this day that Brontes proved himself for all time. He had been working hard, concentrating so fiercely that he didn't even see the naiad. When the fighting started, he simply built himself a wall of anvils. Sheltered behind his iron ramparts, he continued to shape the white-hot lump of metal, completely ignoring the wild scuffle that raged about him.

The disappearance of the naiad refueled the wrath of the she-Cyclopes. They boiled out of the crater, rushed to the river, and began to hurl huge boulders into it, hoping to crush whatever naiads might dwell there. They threw in so many rocks that they quite choked the river. But they were still not appeased because they felt that the naiads had slipped away.

Roaming the riverbank, they knocked down trees with their mallets, piled up the fallen trunks and set them afire. They wanted to raze the countryside, but, luckily, it had rained the day before and the flames did not spread. Finally, they straggled back toward the crater, still simmering with rage.

Cronos, hovering above, was very pleased by all this. He knew how badly he had disrupted the work of the smiths and hoped now that they would never be able to complete the weapons destined to defeat him. He was unaware that Brontes, ignoring the whole affair, was working stubbornly, and by this time had finished the helmet of darkness and had begun work on the trident.

51

9

Before the Battle

ronos met with the elder Titans that formed his war council.

"I have disrupted the work of the weapon foundry," he said. "We must now take the offensive before these accursed rebels gain strength."

"Are you perhaps not overestimating them, my lord?" said one elder. "Can they really be considered dangerous? They're only a rabble of young malcontents, aren't they, with no real support?"

"Very real support," said Cronos. "The Cyclopes are peerless smiths and savage brawlers, and the hundred-handed giants would be sufficiently dangerous one-handed. Both tribes were delivered from captivity by Zeus and would follow him through fire."

"They may have to," said a Titan named Atlas.

"What do you mean?"

"I mean that your son's expedition underground was not wholly a triumph. He freed the Cyclopes and the giants, true, and they are strong allies. But in freeing them, he managed to offend those who are even more deadly. I speak of dragon-kind. Zeus humiliated the entire breed by seizing one of their chieftains and using him as a tool, a torch— a *thing*, in fact. Dragon-kind, I say, has declared itself an enemy to Zeus and his brothers and sisters. And a legion of these armor-plated, spike-tailed, fire-breathing monsters stand ready to fight on our side. I can vouch for them. I have been underground myself, getting to know the beasts."

"That settles it!" shouted Cronos. "We attack immediately. You, my good Atlas, shall be our battle chief."

"Thank you," said Atlas. "My dragons will make a living bonfire of your enemies."

"It is the Titan Helios who drives the chariot of the sun. . . . To steal a spoke of that wheel we must stop the chariot in its journey across the sky."

Zeus went to the smithy. "Lord," said Brontes, "we have finished the helmet of darkness and the three-tined staff. But we have not been able to finish your thunderbolt, for we lack the most important ingredient."

He held up a marvelously wrought zigzag lance of polished iron, volt-blue, radiant. Held aloft in the Cyclops's huge hand, it seemed aflame with energy, and branded the shadows just as a lightning bolt brands the sky.

"It's beautiful," cried Zeus. "Give it to me!"

"Not yet," growled Brontes. "It's not finished."

"What does it lack?"

"The magic fire. A spoke of the First Fire, which must be taken from the sun wheel itself."

"There's plenty of fire right here," said Zeus. "Your forge fires, the smoldering volcano flames that spring from the white-hot core of the earth."

"Not hot enough, not hot enough!" roared Brontes. "We have tried tempering your bolt in these fires, and they are not hot enough. We need a spoke of the sun's fire, I say. To that primal blaze our volcanic fires are only embers, feeble embers."

"Impossible," said Zeus. "It is the Titan Helios who drives the chariot of the sun. The flaming disk we see in the sky is its near wheel. To steal a spoke of that wheel we must stop the chariot in its journey across the sky. And that journey has never been interrupted since the beginning of Time."

"You must do it, my lord, or we cannot finish your thunderbolt."

"And without that bolt, I cannot vanquish my father," said Zeus. "Brontes, we'll need a net strong enough to snare the sun chariot as it races across the sky, yet light enough to float slowly down when cast off a mountaintop."

"My lord," said Brontes, "I can draw out strands of copper into wire so fine that it will be transparent."

"But will a mesh spun from such a wire be strong enough to hold the plunging, bucking sun steeds?"

"How long must they be held?"

"Long enough for someone to steal a spoke of the First Fire from the wheel of the sun chariot. As long, say, as it would take you to chew the roasted flesh off the thigh bone of an ox."

"I get very hungry working like this. I eat fast. Can anyone steal the fire that quickly?"

"Can you make such a mesh—so light and strong?"

"As a spider spins a web to hold a hornet."

"Start spinning," said Zeus. And he strode out of the smithy. Hera hurried after him.

"What is your plan?" she said.

"Helios is a very good charioteer. Once he has begun his journey across the blue meadow of the sky, he never reins up his horses, no matter what. But he also has a strong taste for nymphs. I have seen him chasing them at night, once his horses are stabled. My idea is to get a beautiful naiad or dryad up there somehow, distract him long enough to cast the net over the chariot, and hold it still until I can steal a spoke from the sun wheel."

"I know who's perfect for the job," said Hera. "That leafy vixen who mixed the vomitous drink for our father."

"My dear Hera," said Zeus. "Your beauty is matched only by your intelligence. I'll go find her immediately."

"It is I who will go find her not you, oh fiancé. For I know well that your own partiality for nymphs is at least as strong as the charioteer's."

10

Different Fires

n those first days before man was planted on earth and the gods had only each other to play with, four Titans managed the winds. Since there were no people yet, there were no ships to capsize, no walls to blow down or roofs to blow off, and no fishing villages to sweep into the sea. When the wind Titans raced each other across the sky, tunics fluttering, looking for mischief, they had to be content with smashing trees or piling up waters and hurling them at the empty shores. Once in a while, they charged each other, colliding, darkening the sky, then whirling in a wild dance called the hurricane, trying to catch their brothers and sisters out in the open and blow them away.

Cronos, who disapproved of trouble he did not make himself, forbade the wind Titans to dance the hurricane too often, and they had to live more harmless lives than they preferred. So they were delighted when Cronos prepared for battle and gave each of them work to do.

Boreas, a big blustering brute,
flew over the arctic wastelands.

Boreas, a big blustering brute, flew over the artic waste-lands, filled his lungs with icy breath, and hovered in the sky north of Olympus.

Eurus flew over the swamplands, drew in a great chestful of malarial airs, then flew back to his station east of Olympus. .

Zephyrus, the best-tempered of the wind brothers, did not like to harm anyone but did like to bowl swiftly over the sky and whirl and dance. Hovering west of Olympus, he looked for fine sport in the coming battle.

Notus, who seemed the sleekest and mildest of the four, was perhaps the most dangerous. Striped with strange changeable airs, he would blow a hot sirocco at one moment and a freezing blast the next, making it impossible to live in his domain when his mood turned ugly. He lurked south of Olympus.

While the wind Titans waited in their battle positions, Zeus gathered the young gods about him on a section of slope that was studded with boulders. "Brothers, sisters," he said, "we must fight before we are ready. We face an army of Titans, skilled warriors every one, and enormously strong, while we command only a small band of giants and those few Cyclopes who can be spared from weapon making. Cronos knows about our magical weapons; he knows that they are unfinished yet and that without them we cannot win. That is why he is attacking now."

"Why fight before we're ready?" said Hades. "Why not avoid battle until we are?"

"We cannot avoid battle," said Zeus. "We are trapped in this valley. The Titans will charge down the slope of Olympus and the surrounding hills. But let us not be downhearted. The Cyclopes are working furiously. If we attack first and drive the Titans back, we may receive our new weapons before nightfall. And now, let the battle begin!"

He whistled three notes. Each of the twenty giants seized a boulder in each of his hundred hands. Whirling their long arms, the giants hurled the rocks uphill toward the brass armor of the Titans, which glittered in the sunlight. The Titans were amazed when rocks began to rain down on them as if dropping from the sky. The heavy boulders fell, squashing them like beetles in their brass armor. The young gods yelled exultantly and followed the giants uphill. The Titans broke ranks and fled.

Cronos, who was standing on the very crest of the hill, holding the great scythe that he had used to butcher his father, stood motionless under the shower of rocks. He raised one hand and waved it in a circle.

It was the signal the winds had been waiting for. They bowled terrifically across the sky from the north, east, south, and west, caught the arching rocks, clenching them in mighty fists of air, and blew them downhill, right back at those who had thrown them.

The giants had to stop throwing because they could not stand up under the deadly hail. They were forced to crouch among what rocks were left.

As soon as the last rock had been blown downhill, Zeus sprang to his feet and shouted: "Clubs! Clubs!"

The giants rushed to a grove of trees, uprooted them, and charged uphill. Holding their terrible cudgels, they raced toward the Titans.

Cronos could not call upon his winds to blow the giants away, because the Titans were going downhill and they would have blown away, too.

Cronos signaled. A trumpet sounded. The Titans halted and stood fast halfway down the slope.

Now Atlas, who had been held in reserve, came slowly down the hill. The young gods gaped at him. He was the largest of the Titans, taller than a cedar, which is the tallest tree in the forest. Behind him he seemed to be dragging a train of mossy logs. As he came closer, the young gods saw not logs but green, scaly dragons slithering after him, blowing blue puffs of flame.

Atlas stopped and the stream of dragons parted around him. The puff-balls of flame became jets of flame. The dragons crawled downhill spitting red fire at the giants. The fire hit the trees, and they became torches in the giants' hands. The giants hurled the blazing trees at the dragons. The young gods cheered, but the trees bounced harmlessly off the armor-plated beasts, who kept coming, their gaping jaws like open furnaces sending out gusts of flame.

Hera groaned as she saw a giant catch fire. One hand was aflame, then another, then his arms. He was a wheel of fire. He screamed in agony. Two more giants turned into blazing wheels—whirling, screaming. The giants broke ranks and ran downhill pursued by flame. The coldhearted young gods who so rarely wept felt their cheeks strangely wet as they watched one dragon pause to eat a roasted giant.

"Where is Zeus?" whispered Hades to Poseidon.

"I don't see him," said Poseidon. "Can he have left the field?"

"He's not here," said Hades, "I don't see him anywhere. The coward has fled."

"Never!" said Hera.

"Where is he, then?"

"It's too late in any case," said gentle Hestia. "We seem to be surrounded."

Indeed, they were. A brass wave of Titans was rolling down the hill. When they turned to flee, the young gods saw that dragons had cut in back of them, blocking all retreat.

"Halt!" yelled a great, clanging voice.

The Titans halted. Atlas waved back his dragons. The young gods stood motionless, frozen in horror. Striding downhill

The Titans were amazed when rocks began to rain down on them as if dropping from the sky.

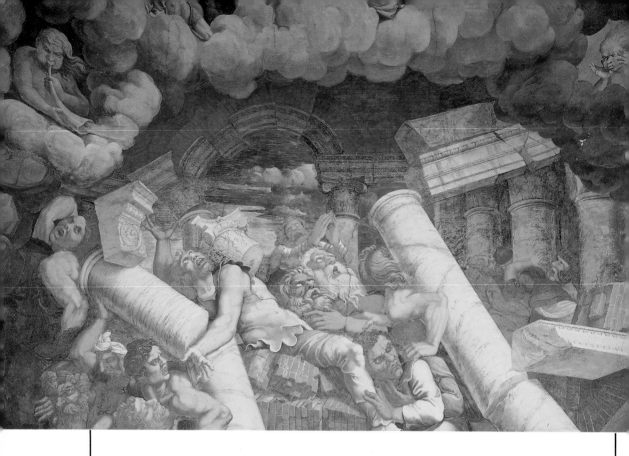

The winds caught the arching rocks
. . . and blew them downhill, right back at those who had thrown them.

was the awful figure of the father who had once devoured them. Coming toward them, holding his sickle high so that the deadly blade flashed in the sun, he seemed like the arch-destroyer of the world, ready to dismember and swallow them again.

A hush had fallen on the field. Not a sound was heard but the faint crackling of a tree set ablaze by a dragon's breath. Cronos came closer and closer yet, smiling a ghastly smile. His blade whisked out and sheared off a lock of Demeter's wheaten hair. She was brave, the tall young goddess. She stood there, chin lifted, her eyes trying to look steadily into those of her father, but when she met the blankness of his eyes, she had to look away.

Poseidon backed away slowly, until he felt the scorching breath of a dragon and had to stop. Hades sank to his knees, gibbering with fear.

"Please, father," said Hestia. But when she heard the softness of her own voice, she realized how useless it was to plead and fell silent.

Hera, the youngest daughter—the youngest of all there now that Zeus was gone—said nothing and did not stir. She felt her fingers curving into talons. "Let him try to swallow me," she said to herself. "I'll claw out his gizzard on the way down."

Cronos must have felt a gust of her hatred. He stopped smiling. An arctic light of pure gray murder glimmered in his eyes. Towering above his children, he raised his sickle.

A strange sound was heard. And those on the slope of Olympus that day saw a marvelous thing. The sound they heard was the wild, eerie mirth of a goat cry, but loud enough to fill the heavens. And what they saw was a goat leaping toward them—a goat bigger than a stag, white as cloud fleece, and with horns silver-gold as the crescent moon. More wonderful still, Zeus was riding her.

He was shouting, laughing, and holding something high. Hera saw that it was a shaft of polished metal, zigzag, radiant with energy. She realized that the Cyclopes, laboring in their crater, had finished the magic weapons.

Climbing up the hill were a horde of Cyclopes coming to join the battle. The goat leaped high, clearing the wall of dragons, and landed among the young gods. Cronos retreated slowly, his sickle still poised.

"Titans, charge!" he shouted. "Atlas, send the dragons!"

The Titans leveled their huge spears and charged downhill toward the young gods. The dragons slithered uphill, jaws agape, teeth wet.

But Zeus had handed Hades a helmet and Poseidon a three-pronged staff. When Hades put on his helmet, he spilled darkness the way a squid spreads its inky blackness through the waters. Darkness washed over the slope of the mountain, covering everything. No one could see anyone, friend or foe. But suddenly, the darkness was pierced by flame as the dragons spat fire. Red flame scattered the shadows. The Titans could see the young gods and resumed their advance. The dragons came at them from behind.

Poseidon raised his trident. He didn't know what it could do, but knew it was his, profoundly his own. He felt a weird power arching from each of its three prongs, streaming toward the sea, pulling at the tides—pulling at him, exerting an enormous claim, attaching him to the sea forever and making him glory in the attachment. He twirled his staff now, pulling the tides up to him as a fisherman gathers his nets. The sea that washed the shore beneath the Olympian cliffs piled up now, higher and higher, its taut waters shining like silk with a pent force, curling into a giant breaker. The wave broke, washing over the slope and dousing the dragon fires. Poseidon lowered his staff.

The waters withdrew, rolling off the mountain. The fires were quenched, but the dragons were still huge beasts whose teeth were like ivory knives, with tails that could flail down stone

*The coldhearted young gods who so rarely wept
felt their cheeks strangely wet as they watched one
dragon pause to eat a roasted giant.*

Zeus shouted. . . . He raised his zigzag bolt. . . .
It was a spoke of the First Fire.

walls. And now Atlas was charging toward the young gods, followed by the great lizards.

Zeus shouted; his voice was thunder. He raised his zigzag bolt; it became a spear of fire—white-hot, blue-hot, primal flame. It was a spoke of the First Fire, the very fire that brands the sky in a thunderstorm. The flame streamed out of his spearpoint, impaling Cronos and nailing him to the rocky hillside.

When this happened, everything changed. The Titans felt themselves dwindling, felt privilege ebbing from their pores. The dragons turned and scuttled away like little lizards, trying to burrow under the rocks. Atlas tried to hide, but he was too big. The Cyclopes leaped upon him, wrapping him in chains.

Other Cyclopes came to where Cronos was nailed to the hillside. Brontes held the net he had made—that wonderful net that had snared the sun chariot. He cast it over Cronos, who struggled helpless as a fly in a spider's web. For the power had passed from him, passed to his youngest son, Zeus, now king of the gods.

11

To Death and Back

eus celebrated his victory by conferring powers. He named Hades Prince of Darkness, King of the Land Beyond Death. Poseidon he made God of the Sea and all therein.

Demeter, whose name means barley mother, he made Goddess of the Harvest, holding domain over all growing things.

Hera appointed herself. Insisting on immediate marriage with Zeus, she took her place as queen of the gods.

It was a puzzle what to do with the eldest sister, Hestia, who disliked court life and conspiracies and battles. Then Hera had an idea that she made Zeus think was his. He made Hestia Goddess of the Hearth and bid her prepare for the coming of a new breed calling themselves humans, who would worship her through marriage.

Zeus, of course, reigned over all. Lord of the Sky, Sender of Rain, he was permanently endowed with a voice of thunder and a lightning shaft.

After he had rewarded the victors, he punished the losers.

Cronos was locked away in a corner of Hades' realm called Tartarus. The Cyclopes were instructed to cast walls of iron to pen him in. The hundred-handed giants were ordered to patrol these walls and make sure he did not escape.

Atlas was punished most severely. As big as a mountain, he was given a mountain's task. He was condemned to stand on the western rim of the world holding a corner of the sky on his shoulders and to bear that unbearable weight through eternity.

Zeus stripped the wind Titans of their powers and gave the management of the four winds to the youngest of the Titans, who, he knew, was too lazy ever to rebel. The name of this new Keeper of the Winds was Aeolus.

He punished only those Titans who had been leaders in the

Zeus pardoned the others and invited them to become part of the glittering court at Olympus.

war against him. He pardoned the others and invited them to become part of the glittering court at Olympus.

As for the Cyclopes, although Zeus honored them for their mighty services, they knew they would never fit into the society of gods and Titans. They were too ugly. Even those who respected them couldn't bear to look at them. So they returned to their smithy to make tools and weapons and ornaments, and everyone was glad they were elsewhere.

There was another reason for the Cyclopes' unpopularity. Although Zeus was no bloodthirsty tyrant like his father and his grandfather, he did wield absolute power and his power resided in his thunderbolt. With that volt-blue zigzag shaft he could gaff anyone like a fish—god, demigod, or mortal—and there was no way to hide from or defend oneself against that spear of fire. His subjects, gods and Titans alike, feared him too much to permit themselves to feel even secret resentment. But they had to blame someone for their fear, so they chose to hate the Cyclopes, who had forged the dreaded thunderbolt for Zeus.

This smoldering hatred brought the Cyclopes into myth again centuries later, after humankind was planted on earth. Apollo, the Sun God, Lord of Music and Healing, loved a princess of Lapith who would not accept his love. Nevertheless, he paid her ardent attention, wooed her with sunstroke, and melted her resistance. When the princess, whose name was Coronis, found she was pregnant, she rebelled and returned to her first love, an Arcadian youth with cool hands.

Apollo's sister, Artemis, always watchful of his honor, was enraged by this and killed the girl with one of her silver arrows. Asclepius was born during the princess's death throes. It is said that the infant, who was to become the father of medicine, watched the details of his own birth with profound attention, displaying a precocious talent for anatomy.

Indeed, he became such a marvelous doctor that he could bring the dead back to life. Hades, ruler of the underworld, complained to Zeus that the young physician, by robbing him, was

Apollo's sister, Artemis, always watchful
of his honor, was enraged . . . and killed the girl
with one of her silver arrows.

attacking the dignity of all gods, and, like an experienced plaintiff, he reinforced his complaint with a huge bribe. Zeus nodded, took up a thunderbolt, and hurled it at Asclepius, killing him. Apollo mourned his son. He was maddened by grief, but not mad enough to attack Zeus. Instead, he stormed down to the crater and shot off a quiverful of his golden arrows, killing every Cyclopes who labored there, making thunderbolts.

Then Apollo went to Zeus and pleaded his son's case so eloquently, in so musical a voice, that Zeus recalled the young physician to life. In return, Asclepius patched up the Cyclopes, who returned to their anvils.

But some of them had learned to hate the gods.

12

Ulysses and the Cyclops

he seeds of Ulysses' most terrible adventure were planted long before he was born—in fact, before the first man was put on earth. It began on that day when Cronos sent the naiad to start a riot in the smithy and disrupt the Cyclopes' weapon making.

This trick of Cronos' was to bear other consequences—to destroy shiploads of men as yet unborn, and to darken the name of the Cyclopes forever. For among the smiths was a youth named Polyphemus, the biggest and most powerful of all, who fell violently in love with the naiad. He couldn't work. He couldn't sleep, he couldn't think of anything but that nymph, white as a birch on the anvil, casting a riverine fragrance upon the sooty air.

He fought his way through the riot in the smithy and rushed to the river. Hiding himself in the reeds when the female Cyclopes came raging down, he waited until they had trooped back to the crater. Then he began to search for the naiad. In his madness he actually began to clear the riverbed, hurling aside the heavy boulders as if they were pebbles.

Now, as it happened, all the naiads had escaped the attack of the she-Cyclopes by simply gliding underwater into a side-stream. But our naiad, whose name was Leuce, came back to the spot on the riverbank where she had first met Cronos, hoping to meet him again and claim a reward. She came in the hour before dawn when it was still dark. In fact, it was darker than it had ever been before because Cronos, who was preparing for battle, had decided to quench the moon that night. The naiad couldn't see anything, so she listened very hard. She heard odd sounds: the grating of boulder being lifted from boulder, and the thump when it fell. She turned to flee, but then caught a scent that reassured her—the scent of a male.

"What are you doing?" she called.

"Looking for you," said a deep rumbling voice.

"For me? Do you know who I am?"

"I do."

"But you can't see me."

"I know you in the dark."

"How sweet. Why are you looking for me under there?"

"Don't you live in this river?"

"Not now. You have such a nice voice. I wish I could see you. I wish the moon would come out. Wait. I'll do like a blind person."

She reached out and ran her hands over his chest and shoulders. She could reach no higher than his chin. "Oh my," she murmured, "you're very big and strong, aren't you?"

"I guess so."

"Are you a Titan? You must be."

"Not exactly. A kind of relative."

"I know you're gorgeous. I can't wait to get a look at you. But it'll soon be dawn."

"Yes."

"Chilly here. Couldn't you hug me or something?"

He took her into his arms and, despite his wild hunger, was

so stunned by love, so confused by joy, that he cradled her in his mighty embrace as though she were an infant. He didn't dare kiss her. He didn't want her to know his face, not until she had seen him for what he was.

The sky curdled, seeping pink light. It fell upon the riverbed, painted the giant figure on the bank holding the birch-white nymph. Her scream split the air. She slid from his arms.

"Your eye!" she cried. "What happened to your eye?"

"Nothing."

"Where's the other one?"

"This is all I have."

"And look where it is! It's in the wrong place!"

"I'm a Cyclops," he muttered. And he reached for her.

She shuddered away. His arms dropped. She vanished into the mist.

> *Polyphemus couldn't work. He couldn't sleep.*
> *He couldn't think of anything but that nymph.*

Utter pain took him. He raised his hand to pluck out the offending eye and crush it under his foot like a snail. But with the impulse to violent action, his grief mixed with rage. He decided to fling himself outward into the world, never to return to the hated forge. He strode away from the crater, through a forest to the sea.

It is told that other young Cyclopes joined him and insisted on going wherever he went, for he had always been a leader among them. They knocked down trees and lashed them together to make a great raft. Using their mallets as paddles, they stroked so powerfully that the clumsy raft skimmed over the water like a canoe.

They finally came to an island that suited Polyphemus. Hilly and heavily wooded, it was inhabited only by wild boars, wild goats, and fleet red deer. "This is it!" cried Polyphemus. "We'll hunt and fish and never touch an anvil again."

They did indeed live that way and, as time passed, became very different from what they had been. Without their own work to do, their talents rusting, they sank into bestiality. Polyphemus, their leader, led them there also. With the most to lose, he lost the most. For, lurking behind all thoughts and memories was the image of the nymph who had touched him in the dark and fled at dawn. His companions fished for sea nymphs and occasionally caught one, but he couldn't bear to. He never again wanted to see that look of horror upon a nymph's face. Instead, he cultivated only his appetite for food until he became one gross hunger. Worst of all, he developed a taste for human flesh.

It happened one stormy day that a ship was driven onto shore and split upon a rock. The Cyclopes, who had become magnificently strong swimmers, dived in and hauled out the drowning sailors. But the swim had made the Cyclopes very hungry, and the day was still too stormy for hunting.

"They'd have drowned anyway," said Polyphemus. "Look at 'em. They're half-dead. We'll just finish them off and have us a hot meal."

He took a sailor in his huge hand and twisted his neck like a chicken. The others did the same, and grilled the sailors over an open flame.

Now this ship's crew had come from an eastern land where olives grew, and dates and figs. They were young and plump and had a delicate, oily flavor. Polyphemus ate greedily and waited for the next shipwreck.

But the wind stayed fair; no ships were driven onto the rocks. His hunger grew and his temper became so savage that the other Cyclopes began to avoid him. He squatted on the headland and waited for a sail . . . and waited . . . and thought to himself: "Can't wait forever. I'll have to push things along."

The next time he saw a sail in the distance, he swam to the ship, capsized it, and swam back to the island with his pockets full of sailors. This happened again and again until word spread around the ports, and ships began to avoid those waters altogether. Polyphemus had to go without human flesh for a year and a day.

By this time, men had grown civilized enough to fight wars, an activity that the gods found immensely entertaining. They took sides, bet with each other on who would win, arranged ambushes and hand-to-hand duels, and pulled every trick possible to help their favorites, puzzling the warriors, who in their ignorance gave the name luck to this god play.

Now the biggest and bloodiest of these wars had just ended, leaving the gods very bored. One goddess in particular was not only bored, but angry. She was Artemis, twin sister to Apollo and Goddess of the Moon. She and her brother had wagered heavily on the losers. One moonlit night, flying over the Middle Sea in her swan chariot, she spotted a ship that looked familiar. She flew down closer.

"It's Ulysses!" she said to herself. "It's that slimy trickster who did more to defeat my Trojans than anyone else."

She immediately began to plan a disaster, something she could do well, for it was she who swung the tides. "What shall

I do?" she said to herself. "Guide them into a riptide and sink their ship? No, drowning's too easy and there are no sharks in the area. I want something slow and painful for Ulysses. I want him to suffer just as he made me suffer watching my Trojans being tricked by that accursed wooden horse, watching that beautiful city being sacked and burned. Let me think of something really foul."

Her hair and bare shoulders were one color, silver brown, moon-brown, as she leaned out of her chariot to swing the tide on a silver leash and guide Ulysses to the island where the Cyclopes dwelt.

Now during the time when Polyphemus was happily capsizing ships and eating their crews, he had dug a fire pit in his cave and hung a turnspit over it, for he liked his meat browned evenly on all sides. Crouched at the pit was a curly-haired cabin boy whom Polyphemus had not eaten because he needed someone to tend the fire and turn the spit. He also liked to wipe his greasy hands on the boy's curls. But by this time, he so hungered for human flesh that he had decided to have the boy for dinner this very night.

He lifted him by the nape of his neck and held him in front of his face. The terrified lad saw the huge round red eye glaring at him, and tried not to look at the great wet mouth with its yellow fangs. "Only skin and bones," snarled Polyphemus. "Can't roast you; there won't be anything left. Well, bones make soup. Go ahead, useless, fill the pot with water."

He put the boy on the floor and went to the door of the cave—and couldn't believe his eyes when he saw meaty-looking men climbing the hill. It was almost evening; the light was fading. He pivoted the door of the cave, which was an enormous slab of stone, casting a faint glow of firelight upon the dusk. Then he went back inside.

He didn't have long to wait. The men were cold and hungry; they broke into a run when they saw the inviting glow. Ulysses tried to stop them, but they paid no heed. They raced up the

Artemis guided Ulysses to the island where the Cyclopes dwelt.

hillside and into the cave. Ulysses drew his sword and followed.

His heart sank as he saw the great fireplace and the enormous soup pot, for he realized that whoever lived in this cave was very, very big. He heard a rumbling sound and raced back to the door of the cave, only to find it blocked by a boulder. There was no way to get out.

The end of the cave was dark. Far above him he saw what looked like a huge red lantern, and then he heard a loud, grating voice. "Welcome. Welcome. You're invited to dinner, all of you." Something splayed out of the darkness toward him. Fingers! As big as baling hooks. He felt them clamp around his waist, felt himself rising toward the great lantern.

The lantern was a huge, bloodshot eye. Under it was a great, grinning mouth with yellow fangs. Ulysses shuddered in the stinking gale of the monster's breath. But he never panicked. The greater the peril, the better his mind worked.

"Good evening, sir," he said. "We are honored to accept your invitation."

"Good. Good. You understand who will be the main course, don't you?"

"I do," said Ulysses. "But you know, my men and I have just finished ten years of war and faced death more times than I can count. So we are not easily frightened."

"Glad to hear it, captain. Brave men taste better. Cowards don't have much flavor."

"All I ask, good sir, is that you put me down again. I will explain things to my men, and we shall prepare our souls for the journey to Hades."

"You're a tough old buzzard, aren't you?" asked the Cyclops. "Too tough for roasting, probably. You'll do for the soup pot, though. Meant to use the turnspit boy, but he has to go to work again. I'm starved! I need an appetizer."

He stooped suddenly, snatched at the floor with his other hand, and hauled up a sailor. Ulysses watched, horrified, as the struggling man was lifted to the great wet mouth. He had to keep watching as the monster ate the man raw, clothes and all.

Some say that Ulysses . . . heated his
sword in the cook fire, took the red-hot
blade and stabbed it into the monster's eye.

"Don't really like 'em that way," said the Cyclops. He belched and spat buttons. "Like 'em well seasoned and browned on all sides. Down you go, captain. Speak to your men. I'm going to pick herbs: rosemary and sage, garlic and thyme. We'll do things right tonight, we will. And if you make your men cooperate—not try to hide and make me chase 'em all over the cave—why, I'll be considerate, too. I'll wring their necks nice and gentle first and not roast them alive, even though that improves the flavor."

"I agree," said Ulysses.

Polyphemus set him down, went to the cave door, slid the slab aside, then back, and Ulysses was alone with his men, who were on their knees, whimpering like frightened children.

"Up!" cried Ulysses. "Stand up like men or you'll be devoured like chickens. Up now, up! He'll be back soon. Get yourselves out of sight and stay hidden until I call."

The men vanished into the shadows. Ulysses waited, thinking hard. Something nagged at his mind—a splinter of a tale heard long ago. He began to search the vast, cluttered attic of his memory. As a boy, he had devoured the legends of heroes, gods, and monsters. Ambushing every traveling minstrel who had come to his father's castle at Ithaca, he had demanded more stories, and more, and more. No minstrel could resist the fox-faced, red-headed lad who seemed to listen with his eyes.

Like a tree fledging itself out of the mist, a tale began to take form—an old, old tale told by a green-clad bard—of a river nymph and her monstrous lover. He remembered! The old tale became a new idea, urgent, giving off light and heat as it turned into action. Swiftly shuffling options, he began to work out his plan.

Too soon, he heard the slab grating open and shut. The Cyclops appeared, carrying an armful of greenery. "Where's that

83

boy?" he roared. "C'mon, runt, start chopping." He hurled the
herbs at the lad. "Where are your men?" he said to Ulysses.

"Saying their prayers."

"They'd better say 'em fast. Now you, captain—what's
your name, by the way?"

"I'm called . . . Nobody."

"Well, Captain Nobody, why don't you strip? You're going
into the soup pot."

"I have something very important to tell you, Polyphemus.
I am a surgeon."

"What's so important about that?"

"It's what I can do for you."

"For me?"

"I fix bodies. Cut off arms and legs when they go bad. Sew
up wounds. Mend broken bones. Battlefield repairs, you know.
Useful in a war. You have anything that needs fixing?"

"I have this feeling of hunger, doctor. But I know you have
a cure for that."

"Wait!"

"I've waited long enough. Hop into the pot."

"In your own interest, my friend, you really ought to save
me for later. Give me a chance to fix that eye of yours."

The Cyclops's bellow of rage blew the turnspit boy off his
stool. Before he could rise, Polyphemus drew back his foot and
swung his leg in a mighty kick, lifting the boy off the ground
and sending him into the rock wall. He fell and lay still.

"What do you mean *fix* my eye?" roared the Cyclops.
"Something wrong with it?"

Ulysses knew the monster might kill him on the spot if he
answered directly. "Oh, well," he thought. "I'd just as soon go
quickly as be soupmeat."

"I asked you a question." growled Polyphemus. "Is something wrong with my eye?"

"Well, to start with, you have only half the usual number.
And the one you have is in the wrong place."

"Wrong place?"

"Haven't you noticed?"

Ulysses saw the monster stalking toward him, opening and closing his huge hands; he tried to retreat but his back was against the wall.

"Wait! Wait!" he cried. "What I'm trying to tell you is that I can fix that eye."

"Shut up!"

"Ever hear of Asclepius?"

"No."

"You should have. He's an important part of Cyclopes history."

"Quickly!" whispered Ulysses.
"Swing under the bellies of the goats."

*Ulysses was horrified to see an enormous
hand descending upon his goat.*

"I hate history."

"Listen . . . listen. Asclepius was a son of Apollo, and the best doctor who ever lived. He was the one who brought the Cyclopes back to life after Apollo killed them."

"What history does is make me hungry. And I was hungry to start with."

He looked down at the sprawled body of the boy and turned it over with his foot. "Is he dead, doc? Don't bother looking; he is. So I won't be able to roast anybody because I have no one to turn the spit. Question is: am I hungry enough to eat you raw? Answer is: yes."

"Wait!" shouted Ulysses. "Let me make my point. I am a cousin of Asclepius. Apollo's half brother, Hermes, is my great-great-grandfather. And this is the point: I have inherited the great doctor's skill. I can give you a new face."

"Nobody can do that."

"You'll be absolutely gorgeous."

"Gorgeous. Someone called me gorgeous once in the dark."

"When I get through with you, they'll say it by daylight

or moonlight. No nymph in the world will be able to resist you."

"Won't they?"

"With your physique? Without that inflamed hole in the middle of your forehead? With two glowing, tragic eyes right where they should be? Naiads and dryads will swarm like flies."

"What exactly can you do?"

"Divide that one gross eye in two and put them in the right place."

"Will it hurt?"

"You'll be asleep. You'll feel no pain. I'll fill you full of unwatered wine."

"I've never drunk wine. We drink only ox blood and buttermilk here."

"All the better. It'll knock you out faster if you're not used to it."

Ulysses unslung a flask of wine from his belt and passed it to Polyphemus, who poured it down his gullet in one gulp. Ulysses watched him closely. He saw the great red eye misting over, as when a furnace is banked and gray ash sifts over the coals. But the eye did not close. The Cyclops was awake—blurred but awake.

"Tastes good," he muttered. "Still awake, though. Sure'd feel it if you started cutting."

"You require stronger medication," said Ulysses.

He stepped in back of the seated giant, grasped the haft of his great hammer and tried to lift it. It was too heavy. But his life was at stake, and the lives of his men. Calling up every ounce of his strength, the last tatter of his will, all his desire to get home, all his wish to live—and thinking, "Hermes, grandfather, help me now"—he lifted the mallet, raised it high above his head, and smashed it down on the Cyclops's skull.

Polyphemus fell heavily.

Reports of what happened next in the Cyclops's cave differ widely. Some say that Ulysses kept feeding the monster unwatered wine until he passed out, then heated his sword in the cook fire, took the red-hot blade and stabbed it into the monster's eye.

Another tale says that Ulysses, convincing himself that he really was a surgeon, borrowed needle and thread from his sail-maker and sewed the eye shut as the Cyclops lay in a drunken sleep.

Still another story says that he did indeed practice surgery, that he took a knife and cut the eye out of the Cyclops's head and tossed it into the soup pot.

Of all these tales, it is the sword version that seems most likely, for we have the exact words that Ulysses spoke to his crew: "Six of you stand at one ear, six of you at the other—and hold his head still so I can strike true. I shall try to stab right through his eye into his brain and finish him off. But if I don't, if I only blind him, be aware that he'll arise in agony and thresh about the cave trying to kill us all. If that happens, get yourselves among the goats as fast as you can."

The men took up their positions at each ear. Ulysses pulled a rock to the giant's head, climbed up on it, and looked down at the huge eye, which stared glassily up at him. Ulysses raised his sword in both hands and, murmuring "Hermes, give me strength," stabbed down, driving the red-hot spike into the eye.

The great head rose from the floor as if it were a separate living thing, tearing its ears from the men's grasp. They fell to the floor and scrambled away. Polyphemus was on his feet, screeching, bellowing, and clutching at the bloody hole that had been his eye. He began to stamp around the cave, trying to crush people under his feet. He slapped the walls with great blows of his hand, unfortunately for one man who had chosen to hide in a niche of rock. The fingers found him and tore him to pieces. Ulysses couldn't even hear the sailor's screams because the monster was bellowing so.

Ulysses crawled toward the goat pen at the far end of the cave, motioning his men to follow. They crawled after him and slid among the giant goats just in time, for the Cyclops had stopped bellowing and was listening. He would certainly have

Artemis, riding in her swan chariot. . . dipped low and listened to Polyphemus. . . .
"Poor brute," she whispered. "I promise that
Ulysses shall be punished for what he has done."

heard the men panting and the thumping of their hearts had not the snuffling of the goats hidden smaller sounds.

Then Ulysses saw him go to the door of the cave and swing the great slab aside. He realized what this meant. With the cave open the goats would rush out to crop the grass, leaving the area clear so that the monster could search it thoroughly.

"Quickly!" whispered Ulysses. "Swing under the bellies of the goats."

The men swung themselves under the huge rams, clutching at their wiry wool. The herd moved toward the mouth of the cave and tried to crowd through. Ulysses was horrified to see an enormous hand descending upon his goat, but the hand only brushed over the animal's back and did not search underneath. The herd passed through, still carrying the men.

The giant rushed to the back of the cave and began to stamp and scrabble around the goat pen, bellowing with fury when he found no one. The herd grazed on the slope. Ulysses was dismayed to see a big yellow moon floating in the sky. It was almost as bright as day.

"Stay low!" he whispered. He saw tall shadows moving toward the cave and knew the other Cyclopes must be coming to see what was happening.

"What happened?" they called to Polyphemus.

"I'm blind, blind."

"Who did it?"

"Nobody."

"Oh, an accident! How unlucky."

"Hurry, catch him!" Polyphemus shouted.

"Catch who?"

"Nobody! Hurry!"

"He's gone mad," they told each other.

Polyphemus tried to push through them to catch the men, who he knew would be fleeing toward the sea. But the others packed around him, trying to help him, to stop him, because they thought he had been driven mad by pain.

"Now!" shouted Ulysses. "Follow me!"

They raced toward the beach. Looking back, Ulysses saw Polyphemus break through the crowd and come bounding toward them.

"Faster!" cried Ulysses. "He's coming!"

The men had a head start, but the giant could cover twenty yards at a stride. The Cyclops, who had developed a nose like a wild beast, could smell fear and knew that he was coming nearer. He uttered a shattering roar.

"This way!" shouted Ulysses, as he angled off through a grove of trees. It wasn't a straight line to the skiff, but he knew that Polyphemus would follow them wherever they ran. The plan worked. The Cyclops followed them through the grove; they could hear him crashing into trees and bellowing with fury.

Even so, they were only a few yards ahead when they reached their skiff.

They pushed it into the surf, leaped in, and rowed with all their might. Polyphemus stood on the shore, listening. He heard the oars splashing and the men panting. He scooped up a large rock and hurled it after them. It struck just astern.

They reached the ship, which was riding at anchor—a beautiful sight on the moon-spangled water. They scrambled aboard. Ulysses turned and shouted: "Goodbye, monster, goodbye, fool—drunken, gluttonous fool! If anyone asks you again, it was not Nobody but Ulysses who put out your ugly eye."

Artemis, riding in her swan chariot, heard this taunt. She saw that Polyphemus was hurling a last rock, and she guided it so that it landed amidships, smashing the deck and crushing five of the crew.

She dipped low and listened to Polyphemus, who had lifted his sightless face to the moon and was howling like a wolf.

"Poor brute," she whispered. "I promise that Ulysses shall be punished for what he has done. He shall be visited with storm, shipwreck, and sorcery. And if he ever reaches home, it shall be as a beggar, a stranger, one man alone among enemies."

Artemis, like all gods and goddesses, made more promises than she kept. But she kept this one—and made it all happen to Ulysses just that way.

As for the Cyclopes, there are those that believe that they still labor in the mountains and can be heard there to this day, rumbling and shaking the earth. What we do know is that the earth still quakes and mountains still explode in fire, and nobody really knows why.

Acknowledgments

Letter Cap Illustrations by Hrana L. Janto

Opposite page 1, CYCLOPS, *oil painting by Odilon Redon (1840–1916)*
   Courtesy of Rijksmuseum Kroller Muller, Otterloo
      Photo: Bridgeman Art Library/Art Resource, NY

Page 3, VESUVIUS IN ERUPTION, *oil painting by J. M. W. Turner (1775–1851)*
   Courtesy of Yale Center for British Art, Paul Mellon Collection

Page 4, Detail from "The Soul Exploring the Recesses of the Grave," by
William Blake (1757–1827), from Blair's THE GRAVE, *etched by Schiavonetti*
      Courtesy of Metropolitan Museum of Art, New York, Harris Brisbane
      Dick Fund, 1917 (17.3.2398)

Page 6, THE ANCIENT OF DAYS, *hand-tinted etching by William Blake*
   Courtesy of Library of Congress, Washington, D.C.

Page 8, THE MUTILATION OF CRONOS, *central detail from a mural by Giorgio Vasari
(1511–1574)*
      Courtesy of Palazzo Vecchio, Florence
         Photo: Scala/Art Resource, NY

Page 10, Mask of a father, in New Comedy Mural from Pompeii (50
B.C.–A.D. 60)
      Photo: Art Resource, NY

Page 13, CYCLOPS, *oil painting by William Baziotes (1912–1963)*
   Courtesy of Art Institute of Chicago

Page 16, SATURN DEVOURING ONE OF HIS SONS, *oil painting by Francisco Goya
(1746–1828)*
      Courtesy of Prado, Madrid
         Photo: Art Resource, NY

Page 21, SALA DELLE ASSE, *fresco by Leonardo da Vinci (1452–1519)*
   Courtesy of Castello Sforzesco, Milan
      Photo: Bildarchiv Foto Marburg/Art Resource, NY

Page 22, THE BIRTH OF JOVE, *oil painting by Nicola Grassi (1682–1748)*
   Courtesy of Coll. Fermo Solari, Udine
      Photo: Alinari/Art Resource, NY

92

Page 24, NURTURE OF JUPITER BY NYMPH, *oil painting by Jacob Jordaens (1593–1678)*
> Photo: Kavaler/Art Resource, NY

Page 26, JOVE AND THE GOAT AMALTHEA, *marble sculpture by Gianlorenzo Bernini (1598–1680)*
> Courtesy of Galleria Borghese, Rome
> Photo: Kavaler/Art Resource, NY

Page 29, A HILL PRAYER, *drawing by Maxfield Parrish (1870–1966)*
> Courtesy of Fogg Art Museum, Harvard University, bequest of Grenville
> L. Winthrop

Page 30, Group in Hell, engraving by Niccolo della Casa of nearly destroyed portion of Michelangelo's LAST JUDGMENT
> Photo: Bildarchiv Foto Marburg/Art Resource, NY

Page 32, MEDITATION ON AN OAK LEAF, *tempura, pastel, and sand on canvas by André Masson (1942)*
> Courtesy of Museum of Modern Art, NY

Page 35, AT THE GATES OF HELL, *illustration by the Limbourg Brothers from* TRÉS RICHES HEURES DU DUC DE BERRY, fol. 103v (15th-century mss.)
> Courtesy of Musée Conde, Chantilly
> Photo: Giraudon/Art Resource, NY

Page 36, PRESCIENCE, *oil painting by Roberto Matta (1939)*
> Courtesy of Wadsworth Atheneum, Hartford, CT, Ella Gallup
> Sumner and Mary Catlin Sumner Collection

Page 38, DRAGON, *drawing by Benvenuto Cellini (1500–1571)*
> Courtesy of Musee du Arte Decoritif, Paris
> Photo: Giraudon/Art Resource, NY

Page 40, BACCHUS AND VESUVIUS, *mural from Pompeii*
> Courtesy of National Museum, Naples
> Photo: Scala/Art Resource, NY

Page 43, THE NYMPH OF FONTAINEBLEAU, *bronze statuette by Cellini*
> Courtesy of Louvre, Paris
> Photo: Giraudon/Art Resource, NY

Page 44, ZEUS, *bronze statuette by Cellini*
> Courtesy of Bargello Museum, Florence
> Photo: Scala/Art Resource, NY

Page 46, Corinthian helmet, said to be from Olympia
> Courtesy of Metropolitan Museum of Art, New York, Dodge Fund, 1955
> (15.11.10)

Page 48, BATHER WITH LONG HAIR, *oil painting by Auguste Renoir (1841–1919)*
> Courtesy of Orangerie, Paris
> Photo: Giraudon/Art Resource, NY

Page 50, ARMORER WORKING ON A HELMET, *Corinthian bronze statuette*
> Courtesy of Metropolitan Museum of Art, New York, Fletcher Fund,
> 1942 (42.11.42)

Page 52, OLYMPUS, *ceiling fresco by Giulio Romano (1499–1546)*
  Courtesy of Palazzo del Te, Mantua
    Photo: Scala/Art Resource, NY

Page 54–55, CHARIOT OF THE SUN, *ceiling fresco by Tiepolo (1696–1770)*
  Courtesy of Palazzo Clerici, Milan
    Photo: Scala/Art Resource, NY

Page 58, Detail from THE BIRTH OF VENUS, *oil painting by Sandro Botticelli (1445–1510)*
  Courtesy of Uffizi Gallery, Florence
    Photo: Scala/Art Resource, NY

Page 60, INITIAL WITH BOREAS, from illuminated mss., LIBERALE DA VERONA Cod. 20.5 c. 36 V.
  Courtesy of Piccolomini Library, Siena
    Photo: Scala/Art Resource, NY

Page 63, ROOM OF THE GIANTS, *detail from a fresco by Romano*
  Courtesy of Palazzo del Té, Mantua
    Photo: Alinari/Art Resource, NY

Page 64, THE FALL OF THE GIANTS, *fresco by Romano*
  Courtesy of Palazzo del Té, Mantua
    Photo: Scala/Art Resource, NY

Page 66, Illustration by William Blake from Dante's "Inferno," Canto XXV
  Courtesy of Metropolitan Museum of Art, New York, Rogers Fund, 1917
    (17.65.4)

Page 67, ZEUS HURLING THUNDERBOLT, *Greek archaic bronze from Dodona*
  Courtesy of Museum of Antiquities, Berlin
    Photo: Bildarchiv Foto Marburg/Art Resource, NY

Page 68, THE JAWS OF HELL FASTENED BY AN ANGEL, *from the Winchester Psalter (Ca. 1140–60)*
  Courtesy of British Library, London
    Photo: Bridgeman Art Library/Art Resource, NY

Page 70, THE COUNCIL OF THE GODS, *oil painting by Peter Paul Rubens (1577–1640)*
  Courtesy of Louvre, Paris
    Photo: Scala/Art Resource, NY

Page 72, DIANA OF THE HUNT, *Fontainebleau School*
  Courtesy of Louvre, Paris
    Photo: Art Resource, NY

Page 74, ULYSSES DERIDING POLYPHEMUS, *oil painting by J. M. W. Turner*
  Courtesy of National Gallery, London
    Photo: Bridgeman Art Library/Art Resource, NY

Page 77, POLYPHEMUS, *detail from fresco by Romano*
  Courtesy of Palazzo del Té, Mantua
    Photo: Bildarchiv Foto Marburg/Art Resource, NY

Page 81, JOURNEY OF ODYSSEUS, *ancient fresco*
> Courtesy of Vatican, Rome
>> Photo: Scala/Art Resource, NY

Page 82, ULYSSES BLINDING POLYPHEMUS, *oil painting by Pellegrino Tibaldi (1527–1596)*
> Courtesy of Palazzo Poggi, Bologna
>> Photo: Scala/Art Resource, NY

Page 85, ULYSSES ESCAPES FROM POLYPHEMUS UNDER THE BELLY OF A RAM, *ancient Greek sculpture*
> Courtesy of Palazzo Doria, Rome
>> Photo: Alinari/Art Resource, NY

Page 86, ULYSSES AND HIS COMPANIONS ESCAPE FROM THE ISLAND OF THE CYCLOPES, *fresco by Tibaldi*
> Courtesy of Palazzo Poggi, Bologna
>> Photo: Scala/Art Resource, NY

Page 89, THE MOON AND THE HOURS, *oil painting by Tintoretto (1560–1635)*
> Courtesy of Museo Imp. Federico, Berlin
>> Photo: Alinari/Art Resource, NY

BOOKS BY BERNARD EVSLIN

Merchants of Venus
Heroes, Gods and Monsters of the Greek Myths
Greeks Bearing Gifts: The Epics of Achilles and Ulysses
The Dolphin Rider
Gods, Demigods and Demons
The Green Hero
Heraclea
Signs & Wonders: Tales of the Old Testament
Hercules
Jason and the Argonauts